TAMING
THE
BLACK DOG

Other books by Bev Aisbett

Living With IT
Living IT Up
Letting IT Go
Get Real
Little Book of IT

Bev Aisbett

TAMING
THE
BLACK
DOG

A guide to overcoming DEPRESSION

HarperCollins*Publishers*

Enquiries for Bev Aisbett's workshops should be made to
Anxiety Disorders Assoc. of Victoria (ADAVIC).
Phone: (03) 9853 8089
E-mail: adavic@adavic.org

HarperCollins*Publishers*

First published in Australia in 2000
by HarperCollins*Publishers* Pty Limited
ABN 36 009 913 517
A member of the HarperCollins*Publishers* (Australia) Pty Limited Group
www.harpercollins.com.au

HarperCollins*Publishers*
25 Ryde Road, Pymble, Sydney NSW 2073, Australia
31 View Road, Glenfield, Auckland 10, New Zealand
77–85 Fulham Palace Road, London W6 8JB, United Kingdom
2 Bloor Street East, 20th floor, Toronto, Ontario M4W 1A8, Canada
10 East 53rd Street, New York NY 10022, USA

National Library of Australia Cataloguing-in-Publication data:

Aisbett, Bev.
Taming the black dog: a guide to overcoming depression.
ISBN 0 7322 6757 9.
1. Depression. Mental – Popular works. I. Title.
616.8527

Cover illustration by Bev Aisbett
Printed and bound in Australia by Griffin Press.

70gsm Classic used by HarperCollins*Publishers* is a natural, recyclable product made
from wood grown in sustainable forests. The manufacturing processes conform to the
environmental regulations in the country of origin, Finland.

28 27   09

To Grace, my daughter — who taught me that too many tears would only serve to weigh down her wings

ABOUT THE AUTHOR

Bev Aisbett is the author of three self-help books *Living with IT*, *Living IT up* and *Letting IT go*, which have now helped thousands of people throughout Australia and overseas attain recovery from the crippling effects of anxiety.

Bev has, for the past twelve years, trained extensively in personal development, therapy skills and advanced counselling.

For the past two years, she has conducted the 'Working with IT' workshops — an extensive program aimed to further assist sufferers towards not only recovery from anxiety, but also greater independence, freedom and self-esteem in all areas of their lives.

A past sufferer of both anxiety and depression, Bev now brings her own experience, learning and wisdom to the assistance of people suffering from one of the greatest challenges of modern life — depression, through this book, *Taming the Black Dog*

Contents

INTRODUCTION

I haven't had a very easy life. Like you, I have had a lot of losses and endured a lot of pain.

Sometimes, even now, I will surrender to pain and I will spend a day or two in the miserable company of the Black Dog — DEPRESSION.

I allow him to seduce me, for he offers me the temptation of giving up, of saying 'Too Hard'. He extends to me the luxury of being absolved of all responsibility to address, repair or change my life.

I can even be enticed into thinking that this retreat from life is a kind of relief, a kind of solution, a kind of sanctuary from life.

I can be fooled into thinking that this constitutes a justified protest at the unfairness of the world — 'See how you've hurt me?' 'Aren't you sorry?' — as if this will change anything.

I can even believe that the Black Dog comes and goes as he pleases — that I have no choice and no control over when he will visit or how long he will stay.

But these days, I can only convince myself of this for a short time, for I have looked into the eyes of the Black Dog and seen what he is made of — ILLUSIONS.

And an illusion, once exposed, can never really exert the same power again.

I now know that if the Black Dog comes, I have opened the door and let him in, and if and when the Black Dog goes it is I who have sent him away.

This little book is aimed to make you, too, master of the Black Dog, instead of his victim.

It will show you his tricks and how to take control. This takes time. Sometimes he is very stubborn, but in the end, he just needs someone to show him the way.

It's *your* life, not his. Claim it back — it's precious. There *is* hope, and there is a way, even though you may not see it. You just haven't gotten to that bit, yet. WAIT ...

This, too, will pass.

Introducing—
The Black Dog

The legendary wartime
leader, WINSTON CHURCHILL,
suffered from DEPRESSION
most of his life.

He named his Depression
the 'BLACK DOG'.

Has the BLACK DOG moved into your life?

Has he TAKEN OVER?

How do you TAME him?

This book is a TRAINING MANUAL to help
you TAME YOUR BLACK DOG.

RECOGNISING
THE
BLACK DOG

WHEN DEPRESSION
BECOMES A PROBLEM

Most of us feel depressed from time to time. This is usually linked to changes, losses and setbacks that are part of life.

These may include:

BEREAVEMENT

JOB LOSS

END OF A RELATIONSHIP

PHYSICAL CHANGES/PROBLEMS

TESTS OF ABILITY OR WORTH

SOCIAL PROBLEMS ETC.

Depression associated with such life events, though painful, is usually TEMPORARY and lifts once life returns to normal or a reasonable period of grieving has passed.

Depression may be a problem however, if it is ONGOING and not apparently linked to an OBVIOUS CAUSE.

IS THIS YOU?

Consistently SAD, BLUE, DOWN IN THE DUMPS?

Lost interest in activities you used to find PLEASURABLE?

OVEREATING

OR

LACK of APPETITE?

OVERSLEEPING?
(or early waking)

LESS ACTIVE OR TALKATIVE than usual?

AVOIDING OTHER PEOPLE?

GOOD BOY!

No longer get a LIFT from PRAISE, GIFTS etc?

LOST INTEREST in SEX?

GRRR

LOW SELF-ESTEEM or HIGHLY CRITICAL of SELF?

Less efficient at SCHOOL, WORK or HOME?

Less able to COPE with EVERYDAY ROUTINES?

Difficulty in making even trivial DECISIONS?

Trouble CONCENTRATING?

And sometimes do you find yourself ...

... entertaining MORBID THOUGHTS?

If you are experiencing four or more of these problems on a REGULAR and ONGOING basis, you may have a problem with Depression which will require ATTENTION.

2

WHEN THE BLACK DOG MOVES IN

THE SYMPTOMS OF DEPRESSION

It is very painful living with Depression.

The colour seems to drain out of the world.

The nights seem unbearably long.

Nothing seems to bring comfort — not love, nor concern nor sympathy.

You feel alone, even in a group.

People describe Depression in many different ways, but the most common images are ...

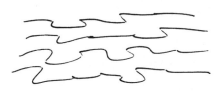

...being lost in a fog

or being pressed down by a great weight.

Some describe

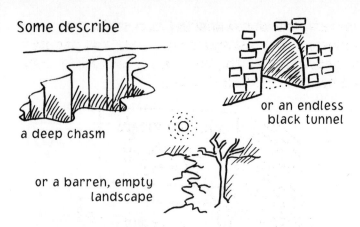

a deep chasm

or an endless
black tunnel

or a barren, empty
landscape

Sometimes Depression may feel like ...

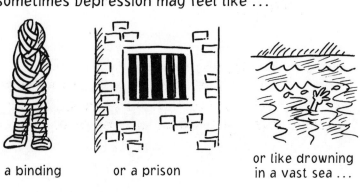

a binding   or a prison

or like drowning
in a vast sea ...

... or the heavy weight, the burden of THE BLACK DOG.

-SIGH-

What these descriptions have in common is a
sense of HOPELESSNESS, a PESSIMISTIC VIEW of the
FUTURE and a deep and lonely feeling of ISOLATION.

But ... YOU ARE NOT ALONE!

In fact, the World Health Organisation has even suggested that a staggering 100 MILLION people are depressed at any one time ... a statistic that may not really CHEER YOU UP!!

However, if we examine this figure more closely, it includes ANYONE who has EVER felt a BIT BLUE, to DEEPLY SAD to INCREDIBLY DOWN, LOST or MISERABLE! (about 90% of us at some time!)

More severe Depression, which seriously affects a person's ability to FUNCTION NORMALLY is rated at about 15% of the population.

The CLINICAL TERMS for Depression include:

REACTIVE OR SITUATIONAL

JOB LOSS

DEATH OF SOMEONE CLOSE

END OF RELATIONSHIP

FAMILY CRISIS

Depression triggered by EXTERNAL events (and therefore usually temporary)

ENDOGENOUS

DNA

Depression believed to be triggered by INTERNAL factors, such as genes or biochemical triggers.

ENDOGENOUS Depression was once believed to be triggered independently from external events.

These days, however, this is seen as not necessarily true. Both can feed each other.

The terms 'REACTIVE' or 'ENDOGENOUS' are now more commonly used to describe the SEVERITY of the Depression.

Causes and triggers are usually a COMBINATION of SEVERAL FACTORS.

These will be explored in following chapters.

Below is a table of different levels of emotional wellbeing. Where do you sit on this scale?

HEALTHY	OUT OF BALANCE	PROBLEMATIC
• Confidence	• Need reassurance	• Sense of failure
• Self-worth	• Self-doubt	• Contemptuous of self
• Creativity	• Uninspired	• Sees no point in anything
• Loving (to self & others)	• Not generous with affection	• Feeling unloved, unlovable & unloving
• Energy	• Low energy	• Depleted energy
• Interest	• Low enthusiasm	• Disinterested in life
• Sexually active	• Lowered sex drive	• Flat-line sex drive
• Socially involved	• Distance from others	• Withdrawn
• Self-motivated	• Needs prodding	• No motivation
• Responsible	• Blames outside factors	• Not looking after self
• Full range of emotions	• Pleasure is compromised	• Feelings of shame, misery and guilt
VERDICT	**VERDICT**	**VERDICT**
OK! STAY!	*TRAINING REQUIRED!*	*UH OH! DOWN!*

3

FLEAS, FUR BALLS AND MUDDY PAW PRINTS

THE IMPACT OF DEPRESSION

Depression makes an impact on most areas of your life, but few of these can take such a toll as in your dealings with others during this time.

You may already be experiencing difficulties in interacting with others.

Some of the problems you may be encountering could include:

Feeling that the depth of your pain is being TRIVIALISED.

Feeling INADEQUATE and a FAILURE because you ARE depressed.

Feeling GUILTY and UNGRATEFUL for being this way.

Feeling caught between WANTING to be ALONE and feeling REJECTED if you are.

Cut this *OUT!* I'm *FED UP* with you *MOOCHING AROUND* all *HANGDOG!*

Feeling
MISUNDERSTOOD
or MISTREATED.

But most of all ...

Feeling ALONE.

One of the greatest difficulties in all of this is in conveying to others what you are FEELING and having them UNDERSTAND.

An important key here is in understanding the difference between being UNHAPPY (which others may perceive your problem as) and being DEPRESSED (which is how you feel).

WHAT IS THE MAJOR DIFFERENCE?

When you are
UNHAPPY you can
SEEK comfort and
ALLOW yourself to
FEEL COMFORTED.

When you are
DEPRESSED, you feel
unable to do EITHER.

This is one of the TRAPS of Depressed thinking. The gap between what you are FEELING and what others PERCEIVE, can, indeed, contribute greatly to your sense of ISOLATION.

Some examples:

1. FLATNESS

FOR YOU

You no longer find PLEASURE in everyday things. You feel DULLED and FLAT.

FOR OTHERS

Your lack of ENTHUSIASM and NEGATIVITY can detract from others' experience of pleasure, too. They may feel CHEATED.

2. NON-RESPONSIVENESS

FOR YOU

You find it difficult to COMMUNICATE, because your feelings are CONFUSING and PAINFUL and you LACK ENERGY.

FOR OTHERS

Your reluctance to speak up can make others feel they cannot REACH you. They may feel REJECTED

3. LETHARGY

FOR YOU
You feel as though your ENERGY has DISAPPEARED.

And, let's be HONEST ...

FOR OTHERS
Your IMMOBILITY may be seen as LAZINESS or SELF-INDULGENCE.

4. SELF-PITY

FOR YOU
You feel UNWORTHY, GUILTY and FLAWED. You GRIEVE over the life you have lost (or never had). You've lost HOPE. Yes, you DO feel sorry for yourself and feel you have good reason to.

FOR OTHERS
Your tendency to be focused on YOURSELF may be seen as SELFISH. Others may look at your life and wonder WHAT you have to be DEPRESSED about.

All of these things make it difficult for EITHER PARTY to close the gap by REACHING OUT, but REACHING OUT is CRUCIAL.

WHAT _YOU_ CAN DO

As difficult as it may feel, your recovery can only begin by your making a move towards it.

YOU CAN REACH OUT BY:

(A) TALKING IT OUT

Right now, your EMOTIONS are very STUCK.

One way to MOVE them on, is to give them an OUTLET.

Talking to someone FREES UP the STUCKNESS.
It helps THEM understand, too!

(B) GETTING A REALITY CHECK

You are having the experience of being INSIDE Depression looking OUT at life. What you see is FILTERED through Depression. Reality is DISTORTED.

Talking to someone can give you a different view on the REALITY of the situation.

(C) GETTING SUPPORT

There is no SHAME in asking for help with a PROBLEM you can't handle by YOURSELF.

There is NO NEED to feel so ALONE. Don't expect people to MIND READ. TELL them!

IMPORTANT STARTING POINTS:

1. FEELINGS PASS!

Emotions CHANGE.
You are not
actually DEPRESSED
EVERY minute of
EVERY day. It just
FEELS that way.

> **THIS, TOO, WILL PASS!**

2. LIFE IS JUST LIFE.

HOW IT FEELS DEPENDS
ON HOW YOU FEEL.

> **REALITY MAY NOT BE AS IT SEEMS**

3. A PROBLEM SHARED IS A PROBLEM HALVED

☆ Accept that you are NOT QUITE YOURSELF at present.

☆ Accept that you may not have all the ANSWERS.

☆ Accept that you may need a HAND with this.

WHAT OTHERS CAN DO—
(SHOW THEM THIS)

(Once recovered, it's an idea for the sufferer to keep an eye out for these, too).

1. IDENTIFY THE PROBLEM

As a friend or family member, you may be first to notice early signs of Depression. These may include:

☆ Increase in ALCOHOL intake.

☆ IMPULSIVE DECISIONS (e.g. suddenly leaving job).

☆ Increased IRRITABILITY.

☆ LETHARGY or DISINTEREST.

Try to encourage the Depressed person to open up and give them a safe and non-judgemental space to truly express their feelings.

2. ENCOURAGE COMMUNICATION

The Depressed person may be closed up for several reasons:

☆ Feeling ASHAMED or GUILTY.

☆ Denying there is a PROBLEM.

☆ Not wanting to be a 'DOWNER'.

☆ Feeling AFRAID to reveal their FEARS, PAIN or EMOTIONS.

☆ Fearing REJECTION or RIDICULE.

Encouragement,
understanding, love
and patience may be
required for some
time.

3. BE COMPASSIONATE

No matter whether you
think the Depressed
person is JUSTIFIED in
feeling this way, for
him/her it is very REAL
and OVERWHELMING.
He/she cannot just 'SNAP
OUT OF IT'.

Remember: YOU ARE
WELL. — BE PATIENT.

4. HOLD YOUR PLACE

Clarify the difference
between being helpful
and creating a 'VICTIM'
mentality.

COMPASSION is one thing
but getting caught up in
'RESCUING' will help
neither of you move on.

You may end up
constantly looking after
the Depressed person,
while they give up on
trying to help themselves.

5. KEEP THINGS MOVING

Do whatever you can to
keep the Depressed
person ACTIVE and
INVOLVED in life.

You may need to
provide the
MOTIVATION that the
Depressed person
lacks at present.

You may need to be
fairly PUSHY about this.

Try to avoid getting
ANGRY, but NOW and THEN
you may need to express
your FRUSTRATION.

Oh, *POOR PUPPY!*

Assessing your relationship and aiming to IMPROVE it can mean CHANGES all round.

6. ASSESS YOUR PART

Honestly assess whether your relationship with the Depressed person may be part of the PROBLEM.

WITHOUT GUILT ask yourself:

⭐ Do I NEED others to be DEPENDENT on me?

⭐ Is the relationship EQUAL, RESPECTFUL and HONEST?

⭐ Do I EXPECT a lot from others?

Above all, see this current situation as a problem requiring a TEAM EFFORT to work through. ENCOURAGEMENT, FAITH and HOPE from OTHERS, HONESTY and HARD WORK from you, the sufferer. This book will guide the TEAM.

THE BLACK DOG'S OWNER

THE ORIGINS OF DEPRESSION

So how did you come to have a BLACK DOG in your life?

In most cases of EMOTIONAL DISTURBANCE, there is seldom a SINGLE CAUSE but SEVERAL contributing factors that add up over time.

In clinical terms, these are known as —

1. PSYCHODYNAMIC

2. BEHAVIOURAL

3. PHYSICAL

1. PSYCHODYNAMIC WORKS THIS WAY —

In early childhood, BELIEFS about ourselves are created by the way we are treated.

NEGLECT, SHAME, LACK OF LOVE, or even being OVERPROTECTED send strong messages about our worth or ability to handle life.

These BELIEFS in turn dictate the way in which we REACT or RESPOND to stressful situations.

For instance, when CRITICISED, you may REACT by:

GETTING ANGRY

BEING PASSIVE

BLAMING YOURSELF

BLAMING OTHERS

And these REACTIONS will be fed by certain BELIEFS you hold about YOURSELF.

I'm TOUGH!

I just cause TROUBLE!

No wonder I'm in the DOGHOUSE again! I'm such a DUD!

The world has RIPPED ME OFF! The world OWES me!

These REACTIONS and BELIEFS can lead to PATTERNS of behaviour that FURTHER undermine your SELF-ESTEEM as you grow older.

For instance:

Getting ANGRY, BLAMING or being DEFENSIVE with others can make you UNPOPULAR.

Being PASSIVE may mean that you tend to be OVERLOOKED.

Blaming YOURSELF may mean that you do not gain RESPECT.

PSYCHODYNAMIC thus refers to the MIND (PSYCHE) affecting BEHAVIOUR/REACTIONS (DYNAMICS).

2. BEHAVIOURAL

According to this theory you may LEARN unsupportive PATTERNS of BEHAVIOUR (such as being passive) to avoid being PUNISHED or to earn PRAISE.

Over time, this type of behaviour leads you to push down your OWN wants and needs in an effort to CONFORM.

As a result, rather than gaining REWARDS, you will tend to be USED, since you have not learned to set clear BOUNDARIES.

3. PHYSICAL

This theory suggests that you could have been born with a certain brain chemistry or brain structure that could make you more likely to experience DEPRESSION.

Changes in the brain apparently cause dulling of nervous impulses, resulting in Depression.

While chemical imbalance may be a CONTRIBUTING factor, it is unlikely to be a SINGLE CAUSE.

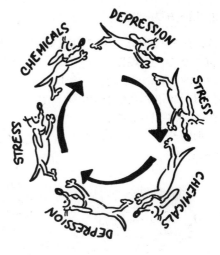

It is still unclear as to which comes FIRST —

CHEMICALS creating MOOD or MOOD creating a CHEMICAL CHANGE!

Regarding GENES, a family history of Depression may be HEREDITARY but it could also indicate LEARNED BEHAVIOUR.

At the very WORST, a GENETIC or CHEMICAL imbalance may make you more SUSCEPTIBLE to FEELING DEPRESSED about life, than others.

THIS IS AN IMPORTANT POINT, SO LET'S EXPLORE IT:

A PREDISPOSITION (chemical or otherwise) to Depression may mean that life may BOUNCE OFF others, but you perceive a PERSONAL BLOW!

If you tend to REACT and RESPOND in a Depressed way, you will PERCEIVE MORE and MORE 'personal blows' which will ADD to your Depression!

THEREFORE

YOU MAY NOT ACTUALLY HAVE MORE HARDSHIP THAN OTHERS, IT WILL JUST SEEM THAT WAY.

Let's take a look:

DEPRESSED RESPONSE

POSITIVE RESPONSE

FINAL OUTCOME?

Let's examine how each dog's EXPECTATIONS and PERCEPTIONS of the SAME SITUATION led to a different EXPERIENCE of it for each.

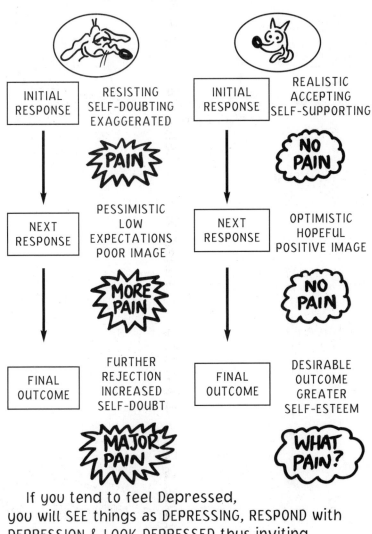

| INITIAL RESPONSE | RESISTING SELF-DOUBTING EXAGGERATED | INITIAL RESPONSE | REALISTIC ACCEPTING SELF-SUPPORTING |

PAIN / NO PAIN

| NEXT RESPONSE | PESSIMISTIC LOW EXPECTATIONS POOR IMAGE | NEXT RESPONSE | OPTIMISTIC HOPEFUL POSITIVE IMAGE |

MORE PAIN / NO PAIN

| FINAL OUTCOME | FURTHER REJECTION INCREASED SELF-DOUBT | FINAL OUTCOME | DESIRABLE OUTCOME GREATER SELF-ESTEEM |

MAJOR PAIN / WHAT PAIN?

If you tend to feel Depressed, you will SEE things as DEPRESSING, RESPOND with DEPRESSION & LOOK DEPRESSED thus inviting DEPRESSING results.

This becomes a VICIOUS CIRCLE.

BUT start out with a DIFFERENT ATTITUDE, and it can become a HAPPY CIRCLE instead! (But we'll get to that, later).

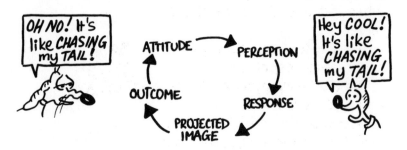

Can you see from this how the three theories —

PSYCHODYNAMIC –	Attitudes from childhood colouring perception
BEHAVIOURAL –	Learned responses to events
PHYSICAL –	Chemical predisposition to depressed response

Can each be contributing to this cycle?

In order to gain a clearer idea of how you have come to feel Depressed, you will need to examine several factors in your life.

These fall into the following categories:

ANY or ALL of these may have played a part in creating your Depression.

🦴 LIFE STORY

(A) CHILDHOOD

What sort of childhood did you have?

Did you feel valued, loved, secure and respected?

Did you learn independence and self-worth?

Issues during childhood that may have affected you include:

LACK OF AFFECTION

Your parents may have been too distant, too busy, undemonstrative or of the 'Children should be seen and not heard' school.

ABUSE

Violent, aggressive or abusive behaviour sends a message to a child that the world is an unsafe, uncaring place.

If violence occurs one minute and 'love' the next, the child will be confused and unsure.

SMOTHERING

On the other hand, if you were overly protected and smothered by affection, you may not have learned true independence and be overly reliant on and affected by others' opinions of you.

HOUSE RULES

An overly strict or disciplinarian household, or a household based on rigid social, religious or ethnic conventions may lead you to be 'obedient' to an extreme or rebellious as a form of protest.

ANYTHING GOES

In contrast to this, an 'anything goes' environment may not have provided you with a sense of structure and security.

While you may not totally fit into these broad categories, as a child you tend to learn by example.

What patterns of behaviour and responses to stress did your parents teach you?

(B) ADULTHOOD

If you were not well equipped in childhood to cope adequately with the many changes and challenges in life, adulthood can indeed be a painful journey.

Your self-esteem, if low to start with, can be further undermined by poor coping skills learned earlier and not adapted to support you over time.

🦴 LIFESTYLE

In contrast to a challenging life, an UNEVENTFUL
life can contribute to Depression, too.

FACTORS HERE INCLUDE:

LONELINESS

BOREDOM WITH JOB
OR DAILY ROUTINE

LACK OF STIMULATING
INTERESTS OR ACTIVITIES

ALIENATION FROM SPOUSE,
PARTNER OR FAMILY

UNEMPLOYMENT

RETIREMENT

TOO MANY RESPONSIBILITIES
— NOT ENOUGH FUN

LACK OF FULFILMENT OR
GOALS

Even normal life events can create accumulated
stress — especially if you don't handle stress well.

In the chart below, tick off the life events you have experienced in the appropriate age bracket, in the colour designated. Red equals high stress.

RED

- DEATH OF SOMEONE CLOSE
- MARRIAGE
- DIVORCE
- MOVING OVERSEAS
- MAJOR DEBT BEYOND MEANS
- VICTIM OF CRIME
- VICTIM OF ABUSE
- JAIL OR DETENTION
- MAJOR ILLNESS/ ACCIDENT
- PREGNANCY/ LOSS OF
- RETIREMENT

ORANGE

- ILLNESS OF SOMEONE CLOSE
- SEPARATION
- CHANGE IN JOB OR POSITION
- CHILD LEAVING HOME
- PERSONAL ACHIEVEMENT
- HOUSE RENOVATION
- QUITTING SMOKING/ ALCOHOL
- LAW VIOLATION
- MOVING HOUSE
- CHANGE OF SCHOOL
- DEBT (MORE THAN $10,000)

BLUE

- BEGINNING/ LEAVING EDUCATION
- FALL OUT WITH FRIEND
- ILLNESS/ ACCIDENT (LONGER THAN 1 WEEK)
- TRAVEL
- DEBT (MEDIUM)
- DIETING
- CHANGE IN SLEEP PATTERN
- FALLING IN LOVE
- JOB INTERVIEW

YEARS	0–5	6–10	1–15	16–20	21–25	26–30	31–35
EVENTS							
YEARS	36–40	41–45	46–50	51–55	56–60	61–65	66–70
EVENTS							
YEARS	71–75	76–80	81–85	86–90	91–95	95–100	101–105
EVENTS							

IT ALL ADDS UP!!

🦴 PHYSICAL

Changes in your body chemistry can also lead to your feeling Depressed.

THESE INCLUDE:

VIRAL INFECTIONS

OVERWORK

HORMONAL CHANGES

INADEQUATE DIET OR
CHANGES IN WEIGHT

OPERATION
OR ILLNESS

PRESCRIPTION DRUGS

RECREATIONAL DRUGS
(AND WITHDRAWAL FROM)

AGEING

If you haven't related to ANY of these, well ...

WELCOME
TO
EARTH!

5

BAD DOG!

SELF-ESTEEM AND DEPRESSION

EVERYONE on the planet is subject to the stresses of daily life — such as

MONEY ISSUES

WORK DEMANDS

RELATIONSHIPS

HEALTH

THE NEED
FOR SHELTER

ADEQUATE
FOOD ETC.

So why is it that some people are able to BREEZE through challenges, while others go under?

The key here centres around an OUTLOOK based on how you feel about YOURSELF.

People will REACT differently to a problem, depending on their attitude to what they feel they DESERVE and their EXPECTATIONS around life.

As we explored in the last chapter, this view is greatly influenced by the messages you were given about your worth when you were a child.

FOR INSTANCE

If you were CRITICISED, IGNORED, TEASED, BLAMED or ABUSED, you will question your VALUE to the world.

You will not expect much JOY from life.

If, on the other hand, you were PAMPERED, SMOTHERED or OVER-PROTECTED, you may not have learned how to be INDEPENDENT. You may EXPECT a great deal from life, but not get it.

If you were BULLIED or RIDICULED for showing your feelings, you may place great WORTH on appearing TOUGH. You may view life with cynicism and anger.

Having to CONFORM, being PUSHED to EXCEL, having to be 'GOOD' may mean that you do not VALUE your own opinions or feelings.
You may see life as OVERWHELMING.

However, if you were NURTURED, SUPPORTED, ENCOURAGED and LOVED you will feel you hold a VALUABLE place in the world.
You will be OPTIMISTIC and REALISTIC about life.

NEGATIVE messages about yourself will tend to create a PATTERN that becomes entrenched as a BELIEF which becomes a REALITY.

In other words, you will tend to BEHAVE according to your BELIEFS about yourself or life.
POSITIVE messages work in the same way, except the PATTERN reinforces SELF-WORTH!

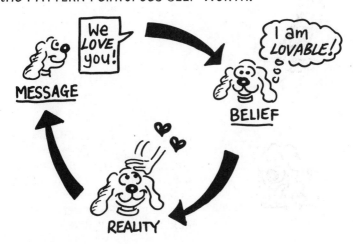

What MESSAGES and BELIEFS in your life have contributed to your current REALITY?

Let's compare the different REALITIES of those with different levels of SELF-WORTH.

Blackie spends a lot of time worrying about what others think of him. He NEEDS to be liked.

Happy does not RELY on others to feel good about himself. If someone does not engage with him, he knows someone else will.

Blackie, feeling unsure of his WORTH, tends to JUDGE others to be BETTER or WORSE.

Happy is not INTIMIDATED by others. He can relax and enjoy them for WHO THEY ARE without COMPARING.

Blackie, needing others' APPROVAL, is ever watchful for signs of REJECTION and cannot RELAX.

Happy is able to DISENGAGE from others' opinions of him. He is thus free to be GENEROUS and EXPANSIVE without fearing being HURT.

Blackie tends to take life's ups and downs PERSONALLY. He also tends to stay focused on the PAIN, rather than exploring OPTIONS.

Happy sees challenges as part of life, but views them as PROBLEMS needing SOLUTIONS. He moves on QUICKLY, so the pain has less IMPACT.

Blackie has trouble setting BOUNDARIES or saying NO. The trouble is, by not setting LIMITS, he feels USED.

Happy only takes on what he WANTS to. Thus he has no need to blame anyone else for his OWN CHOICES.

Blackie avoids taking RISKS or stepping out of a certain model of BEHAVIOUR, for fear of being DISAPPROVED of.

Happy believes that ALL parts of his character are what makes him UNIQUE. He shows his feelings, accepts his mistakes and is TRUE to himself.

Blackie believes that CARETAKING others will make him more VALUED. Others may LET him, but he will rarely be THANKED for it, because it is a form of CONTROL.

Happy leaves others alone to LEARN and GROW from their own experiences. He respects others' RIGHTS to steer their own lives, as THEY see fit, not as HE does.

Low self-esteem is a major factor in your Depression. As you can see from the above examples, it will tend to govern the CHOICES you make which affect the DIRECTION your life takes.

A clear understanding of how this operates in your life is necessary for you to make DIFFERENT CHOICES in the future.

What creates SELF-ESTEEM?

As children, our parents and elders are ALL-POWERFUL figures ... in fact, they are almost GODS. We rely on them for NURTURE, SECURITY and EMOTIONAL care.

They also teach us about LIFE by example.

We seldom QUESTION these teachings because:

(A) We do not have the EXPERIENCE to make comparisons.

(B) We trust in the PROCESS.

(C) We NEED our parents/elders to be RIGHT — for, if not, where does that leave US?

(D) Our very SURVIVAL depends on being LOVED and APPROVED of — i.e. BELONGING.

We will win this LOVE and APPROVAL by various means —

COPYING

A boy sees his father and a girl her mother as the model for being a MAN or a WOMAN. The parent of a child of the opposite gender represents a FIRST LOVE. A child will tend to COPY and DEFEND a parent's behaviour — ANY behaviour!

COMPLIANCE

The child soon learns that certain behaviours are OK and that others are not.
In order to PLEASE (or PLACATE) Mum or Dad, the child will learn to COMPLY.

COPING STRATEGIES

If disobedience means PAIN (emotional or physical) and this pain is constant, the child will firstly become PASSIVE (so as not to upset) then SWITCH OFF EMOTIONS (to avoid feeling pain).

PLAYING THE GAME

Boys don't CRY.
Girls don't LOSE THEIR TEMPER.
If there are RULES that forbid certain EMOTIONS, we may SHUT DOWN on our natural EXPRESSION.

SEEKING REWARD

A child will respond most to what is REWARDED or PRAISED
We may be rewarded for:

- Being OBEDIENT   • Being SORRY
- Being CLEVER   • Being INVISIBLE
- Being QUIET   • Being PASSIVE
- Being GOOD   • Being TOUGH

Many people with Depression will have issues around COMPLIANCE, DEPENDENCY or PASSIVITY.

This PASSIVITY may be disguised under an apparently assertive exterior in some cases, but will be revealed through UNCLEAR BOUNDARIES, DECISIONS BASED ON PLEASING OTHERS, OVER-RELIANCE ON OTHERS' APPROVAL and A NEED TO EXCEL.

If, early on, you learn to be PASSIVE, you may miss out on crucial GROWTH, through RISK TAKING, DECISION MAKING, PROBLEM SOLVING and EXPRESSING OPINIONS and EMOTIONS OPENLY.

'Playing it safe' may mean you end up as a SPECTATOR to life, instead of a KEY PLAYER.

The price we pay for 'ROLLING OVER' may include:

BEING 'USED'

BEING IGNORED

BEING REJECTED

BEING ABUSED

AND ULTIMATELY —

LIFE SUX!

FEELING DEPRESSED!

A WORD FOR THE FOLKS

While much of this chapter has centred around childhood issues, and, in particular, the type of PARENTING you had, this is not to lay BLAME at the feet of your parents!

There are a few things to keep in mind here.

☆ Your parents were also taught by THEIR parents! That's all they knew.

☆ YOU live in a time when you have the opportunity to grow spiritually BEYOND the limitations of the past.

☆ In other words, you can become BIG enough to accommodate another's SMALLNESS.

☆ While your childhood may have been tough, you have a CHOICE as an ADULT to remain that wounded CHILD, or not.

☆ It is IMPOSSIBLE to be a PERFECT parent.

☆ Your childhood can lead to an important decision in your own life — TO DO BETTER!

6

'GIVE A DOG
A BONE'

THINKING AND DEPRESSION

Of course, knowing the CAUSE or CAUSES of your Depression, or even acknowledging that you have LOW SELF-ESTEEM is going to remain little more than an ACADEMIC EXERCISE unless you identify how you 'do' your own particular form of Depression, and CHANGE that!

IN OTHER WORDS — How do you THINK about having Depression, or indeed, LIFE in general?

For instance, if you believe that your Depression is purely GENETIC (or CHEMICAL) in origin, you might THINK about that in several ways.

YOU MAY THINK OF YOURSELF AS A VICTIM.

YOU MAY FEEL HELPLESS AND OVERWHELMED THAT THERE IS LITTLE YOU CAN DO ABOUT THIS THING THAT HAS HAPPENED TO YOU.

YOU MAY DREAM ABOUT BEING RESCUED

OR . . .

O.K. I've got DEPRESSION. What will I DO about that?

You may decide to ACCEPT that you have a PROBLEM and that you will need to explore ways of living with it. This may, for instance, involve MEDICATION, COUNSELLING, a SUPPORT GROUP or RETHINKING YOUR LIFE!

Can you see how the two different ways of THINKING can either ADD to the problem or HELP you deal with it?

Often we have run UNSUPPORTIVE THINKING PATTERNS for many years, without even realising how DAMAGING this can be over time.

Imagine how DAMAGING the following messages can be if you tell them to yourself day after day, year after year.

NO WONDER YOU'RE DEPRESSED!

The BLACK DOG is good at TRICKS — especially
MENTAL TRICKS that can ADD to your Depression
(or ANY of life's problems, for that matter)
Here are some—

1. AWFULISING

You can feel AWFULLY,
TERRIBLY, HORRIBLY
Depressed or Depressed.
Avoid ADDING to your
own discomfort (in ANY
situation!)

2. RESISTING THE
EXPERIENCE

How often do you fight
being where you are,
doing what you're
doing, feeling what
you're feeling?
How well do you
ACCEPT WHAT IS? (And
work from there?)

3. WAITING FOR THINGS
TO CHANGE

Is your Depression
going to MAGICALLY
DISAPPEAR without you
doing anything
DIFFERENTLY?

There's a saying — 'If
you do what you've
always done, you'll get
what you've always
got'.

4. BOGGED DOG

There ARE things you can do (this book will show you plenty) but NOTHING will change until you ACT.

Do SOMETHING — ANYTHING — as long as you make a start.

5. CHOICE

You have CHOICE about EVERYTHING.

You can even CHOOSE to let Depression take over your while life or to build a life that's BIGGER than Depression.

Stay or move on. Just know that you've CHOSEN.

6. EXAGGERATING THE PROBLEM

You may fall into the trap of looking at a lifetime of insecurity, poor decisions, missed opportunities etc etc and deciding that it's such a MESS there's no way you can even start to make a difference.

This thinking will OVERWHELM you.

7. UNDERESTIMATING THE TASK

While EXAGGERATING the problem can hold you back, UNDERESTIMATING the effort involved to improve matters, can set you up for DISAPPOINTMENT. What's taken a LIFETIME to build up isn't going to be fixed by one walk around the block!

8. COMFORT ZONES

Ironically, over time, your Depression is now less threatening than engaging with the WORLD again. Your ESCAPE has become your PRISON.

A tough decision has to be made to step out of your COMFORT ZONE and back into LIFE.

9. SELF-TALK

A dangerous mental trap is the tape that runs constantly in your head and berates you for your MISTAKES, tells you you're a LOSER, or gives you an endless list of RULES about how you, others or the world SHOULD be.

10. EXPECTATIONS

How REALISTIC are your
EXPECTATIONS of how life
should be?

— Should others support
you emotionally, without
you REACHING OUT to THEM?

— Should your boss not FIRE
you if you're not doing the
WORK?

— Should your parents not
COMPLAIN if you mess up
the house THEY'VE PAID
FOR?

— Should your lover STAY
just because you don't
want him/her to LEAVE?

— Should people not DIE
because you would be SAD
if they did?

— Should others respect
you if you don't earn or
demand RESPECT?

7

THE TRAINING BEGINS —
TOP DOG

REASSESSING DEPRESSION

By now, hopefully, you will have a clearer picture of how you came to be Depressed and how the BLACK DOG's tricky thinking ADDS to the problem.

Now you need to ASSESS how you can APPROACH this problem in a new way, in order to HANDLE it better.

What you have on your hands is a BLACK DOG that needs DISCIPLINE, DIRECTION and TRAINING IN NEW SKILLS.

You want your BLACK DOG to FOLLOW YOUR LEAD — not pull you off track!

NO! NOT THERE!

And the only way to do this is to become TOP DOG.

You need to ask yourself —

Who's in CHARGE?

In other words —

Do I rule my life or does
my Depression?
How much of my THINKING
centres around the PROBLEM
instead of a SOLUTION?
Have I allowed my
Depression to TAKE OVER?

If Blackie is in charge, then YOU will need to STEER him back on course.

This will involve adopting a more SUPPORTIVE view of the PROBLEM itself, to keep you on track.

SUCH AS ...

Recovery involves 4 main decisions —

🦴 To WANT to get WELL

🦴 To risk DISCOMFORT to get well

🦴 To be prepared to make CHANGES

🦴 To BEGIN, and then to CONTINUE.

These decisions may appear obvious, but you are likely to stall on any one of them, because they can involve revealing and acknowledging

that there are parts of yourself that are not always noble, and other parts where you have buried old pain.

To make a commitment to recovery, you will need to apply a lot of SELF-HONESTY and a willingness to MOVE PAST that which has held you back thus far.

At this point, it would be good to acknowledge:

Until I face my own Shadow, I will see it in my life.

In other words, you're going to keep tripping up on what you're trying to AVOID.

In POSITIVE terms, this whole process could be seen as simply a means of building up your EMOTIONAL MUSCLE, so that your weak spots no longer cause you injury!

SELF-HONESTY is the greatest EMOTIONAL MUSCLE BUILDER there is. After all, if you keep TRIPPING YOURSELF UP, how can any OUTSIDE factor be of help?

Being honest with yourself may mean OWNING UP TO:

- SELF-PITY

- INACTIVITY

- WANTING TO BE RESCUED

- BLAMING OTHERS/LIFE FOR YOUR SITUATION

- WANTING TO BE LOOKED AFTER

- BEING ABLE TO CONTROL OTHERS.

Whew!

SELF-HONESTY is not easy, but it results in great FREEDOM. By identifying your TRICKS, and removing them, you learn to VALUE and TRUST your INTEGRITY.

IMPORTANT NOTE:

THIS IS NOT ABOUT JUDGING YOURSELF AS 'GOOD' OR 'BAD' IF YOU 'CATCH YOURSELF OUT'.

YOU HAVE DONE WHAT YOU NEEDED TO DO TO SURVIVE.

THIS HAS BEEN THE ONLY WAY YOU KNEW HOW TO DO IT.

THIS IS ABOUT BECOMING CONSCIOUS AND BECOMING REAL AND ULTIMATELY BECOMING STRONG.

So let's look at the four MAIN DECISIONS from a very HONEST point of view.

TO WANT TO GET WELL

Often we say we want to do something when what we REALLY want is something to be done FOR us or for it to just HAPPEN. Recovery requires WORK. Are you READY TO LET IT GO??

RISKING DISCOMFORT

Self honesty can be UNCOMFORTABLE. Getting up and doing SOMETHING, ANYTHING, can be UNCOMFORTABLE. Choosing not to shut down or hide out can be UNCOMFORTABLE. Reaching out, facing old pain, showing your feelings can all be UNCOMFORTABLE.
But your DEPRESSION will only last as long as you AVOID moving on, and through these things.

MAKING CHANGES

If it's NOT WORKING,
find something that
DOES.
If it's OVER, move on.
If it no longer SERVES
you, LET IT GO.
How can you expect a
DIFFERENT OUTCOME if
you repeat the same
MISTAKES?

TO BEGIN AND TO CONTINUE

Just reading this
book will not create
your RECOVERY.
BEGIN. No matter
what, no matter how,
DO SOMETHING.
Then CONTINUE what
you've begun. Once
off won't do it.
If you fall over, BEGIN
AGAIN.
Keep going.
You CAN do it. In
TIME.

GETTING STUCK

So, what sorts of things (from
a self-honesty perspective)
would cause someone to stay,
by choice, in the misery of
Depression? (or any other
misery, for that matter?)

Let's take a (hard) look —

- INACTION MEANS NO RISK OF FAILURE
- YOU CAN BE TAKEN CARE OF
- YOU GET MORE SYMPATHY, LOVE OR ATTENTION THAN WHEN YOU'RE WELL
- IT'S MORE 'INTERESTING' THAN BEING HAPPY
- YOUR DEPRESSION IS LESS PAINFUL THAN THE CHOICES YOU NEED TO MAKE TO FIX YOUR LIFE (e.g. leaving a relationship).

These things can be tough to face, but they represent barriers to your recovery, and to being your true, authentic self, living life as you would want it to be.

If you find yourself falling into any of these traps, consider how CONTROLLED you are by them.

A TRUE COMMITMENT to being well involves a decision to NOT REMAIN where you are, to set a CLEAR GOAL about where you want to be and to DO WHATEVER IS REQUIRED to get there.

Are you COMMITTED? GREAT!

NOW IT'S TIME TO GET TO WORK!

8

FETCH!

GOING FOR RECOVERY

TRAINING your BLACK DOG involves finding
WORKABLE SOLUTIONS to enable you to handle him
better, so that he no longer keeps you STUCK.

Each of the KEY AREAS that we have looked at
in previous chapters can be approached in a new
way, to produce a DIFFERENT ATTITUDE leading to
a BETTER OUTCOME.

These KEY AREAS include:

☆ THE PROBLEM ITSELF

☆ THINKING AND DEPRESSION

☆ CHILDHOOD ISSUES

☆ SELF-ESTEEM

☆ DEALING WITH LIFE

☆ PHYSICAL FACTORS.

Remember our comparison between BLACKIE and
HAPPY?

The aim here is to close the gap in your
current PERCEPTION of things and move you more
in the direction of HAPPY's view of the world.

THE PROBLEM ITSELF

You've probably been viewing your Depression as if it has just 'happened' to you by CHANCE, or through CIRCUMSTANCES beyond your CONTROL.

HAPPY's view

Happy is taking RESPONSIBILITY for the PROBLEM being in his life. He looks for the REASONS why he has this problem.

Take a look at your life, given all the information you have gained so far. Ask yourself ...

- WAS YOUR CHILDHOOD PERFECT?

- DO YOU HAVE GOOD SELF-ESTEEM?

- ARE YOU WHERE YOU WANT TO BE, WITH WHO YOU WANT TO BE?

- HAVE YOU CHOSEN YOUR DIRECTION IN LIFE OR HAVE OTHERS?

- DO YOU GET BACK AS MUCH AS YOU GIVE?

- IS YOUR LIFESTYLE HEALTHY AND BALANCED?

- ARE YOU ABLE TO FREELY EXPRESS FEELINGS?

- ARE YOU ABLE TO SAY 'NO'?
- DO YOU FEEL FREE OF PAST HURTS?
- DO YOU LOOK AFTER YOURSELF
  AS WELL AS YOU DO OTHERS?

If you answered 'No' to even HALF of these questions, wouldn't you say that it is NOT SURPRISING that you feel DEPRESSED?

So instead of taking the view of 'WHY ME?' you could take the view of ...

SOLUTIONS?

☆ Your Depression has simply HIGHLIGHTED existing VULNERABILITIES.
Now they're IDENTIFIED, you can STRENGTHEN them.

☆ Right now, you are having an EXPERIENCE called Depression. If you look at the thinking above, you may realise WHY you are having this experience.
ATTEND to what this experience is asking you to!

☆ Stop FIGHTING where you are. Work on it till you're SOMEWHERE ELSE!

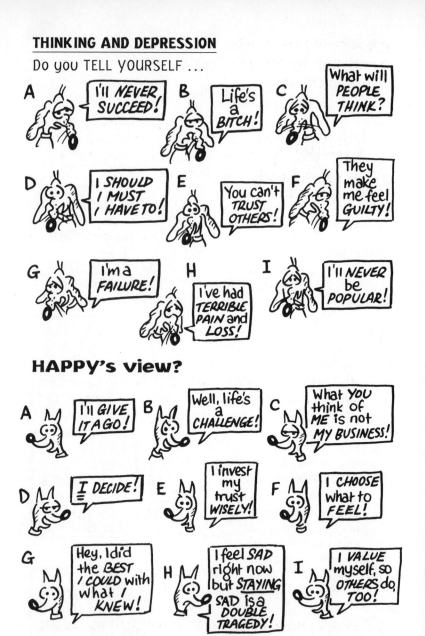

If you really want to be LESS DEPRESSED, then beware of the self-talk that DEPRESSES you!
  Ask yourself this:

- If I want to feel better, can I AFFORD to keep talking to myself in a NEGATIVE WAY?

- Is what I tell myself SUPPORTING or UNDERMINING me?

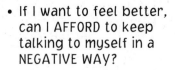

- Would I tell my BEST FRIEND the same messages?

CHOOSE your thoughts with GREAT CARE.
  Thoughts are the FUEL for your emotions. Fill up with DOWNERS and you'll be running on MISERY!

Solutions

☆ Monitor yourself closely for a while. Be aware of what messages you keep running.

☆ If you don't like the station, SWITCH CHANNELS. Challenge the thought. Explore other options.

☆ Omit, as much as possible, all the SHOULDS, MUSTS and HAVE TOs.
  Try 'COULD', 'MIGHT' or 'IF I CHOOSE' instead.

CHILDHOOD ISSUES

You may, indeed, have had a TERRIBLE and TRAUMATIC childhood that still affects you.

HAPPY's view

Happy is saying two things here —
(a) That he has 'GROWN OUT OF' i.e. LEFT BEHIND — his childhood.
(b) He has 'GROWN' BECAUSE OF his childhood — meaning that his early trials served as a catalyst to be BIGGER and BETTER than what he began with.

Solutions?

☆ Refuse to stay LOCKED IN to HISTORY. You cannot change the PAST, but you can change how you view it in the present.

☆ Choose not to engage with others and the world through WOUNDS.

☆ Recognise that, as an ADULT, you can choose to remain a CHILD or not.

☆ LEARN from your past. Do it DIFFERENTLY. Decide to (e.g.) give more LOVE, be more PATIENT, have more SUCCESS than you got before.

PUTDOWNS FROM THE PAST

If part of your self-talk includes PUTDOWNS like these — ask yourself where and from whom these ideas of yourself began.

Happy's view:

Happy has recognised that these putdowns will only cause pain if he BELIEVES them!

Solutions?

⭐ Stop BELIEVING someone ELSE'S opinion of you!

⭐ Stop making these putdowns TRUE!

⭐ Learn to say 'That's THEIR stuff' instead of automatically taking on criticism.

FORGIVING THE PAST

NO!   FORGIVENESS is about FREEING YOURSELF from the effects of the past.

FORGIVENESS IS —

⭐ RELEASING THE PAST

⭐ NO LONGER ATTACHING TO OLD PAIN

⭐ EMOTIONAL CLOSURE

⭐ DISENGAGING FROM ORIGINAL HURT

⭐ ACCEPTING WHAT _WAS_, CAN'T BE CHANGED, BUT WHAT _IS_ CAN.

Happy's view:

Happy has recognised that emotions like SHAME, GUILT, ANGER or FEAR that he may carry from the past keep HIM a VICTIM of the past.

If you think about it, it's pretty strange to torture YOURSELF more than those who originally caused you pain!

Solutions?

☆ Right here, right now, REFUSE to remain a VICTIM of the past.

Here is your statement of FREEDOM

> X, (someone's name) I hereby release you from MY anger, MY pain, MY fear, and MY guilt. Go in peace and so will I.

- Do this little ritual, by yourself, for yourself.

RELEASING THE PAST

- Face one end of a room and imagine before you all of the sad, hurtful painful things of the past, piled one on top of the other. Pile it all up, gather it all together in one big heap.

- Look at that pile of junk and let yourself FEEL all the emotions that come up, let them go, release them. Grieve, weep.

- Now turn and face the other end of the room. This is your future, free of baggage. Embrace it.

SELF-ESTEEM

Self-esteem means you CARE ENOUGH for yourself that you SUPPORT yourself in all your DECISIONS, CHOICES, RESPONSES and REACTIONS.

While this may be simple in PRINCIPLE, getting there can be hard, especially if you've had a lot of blows to your self-worth.

Happy's view:

Happy has figured out that what he GIVES OUT is what he will GET BACK.

Let's look at a few of these —

☆ If you give out HELPLESSNESS you're going to be treated like a CHILD.

☆ If you give out GUILT you'll get back SHAME.

☆ If you give out RESENTMENT, how are you going to get back LOVE?

☆ If you give out MISERY are you going to uplift others? Are they going to ENJOY being with you?

The biggest STUMBLING BLOCKS to self-esteem come from the following —

⭐ OVEREMPHASIS ON OTHERS' OPINIONS OF YOU

⭐ ALLOWING OTHERS OR CIRCUMSTANCES TO DICTATE THE DIRECTION YOUR LIFE TAKES

⭐ NOT SETTING CLEAR BOUNDARIES (i.e.) SAYING 'YES' WHEN YOU MEAN 'NO'

⭐ FEELING THAT THIS IS ALL YOU DESERVE AND NOT SEEKING MORE

⭐ BAD PRESS ON YOURSELF (i.e.) NEGATIVE SELF-TALK etc.)

Let's examine these —

1. OTHER'S OPINIONS

Living your life to please others can NEVER work, simply because it's IMPOSSIBLE to please everybody all of the time.

2. LIFE DIRECTION

No one and nothing can MAKE you do something unless you have AGREED to it on some level.

For example, if you were LIED to, ask yourself 'What do I give out that says it's OK to do that to me?'

3. BOUNDARIES

Agreeing to something you don't want is NOT LOVING.
If you are doing it because you WANT approval or DON'T WANT disapproval, then it is not a gift.
A gift has no price tag.

4. ALL I DESERVE

If you place LIMITATIONS on your life, don't be surprised if your life is LIMITED!

5. BAD PRESS

You're going to LIVE OUT what you TELL YOURSELF.

IMPORTANT THOUGHT —
'We teach others how to treat us'.

Solutions?

☆ See others' approval as a BONUS not a NECESSITY.

☆ Take full responsibility for your OWN life. Live it how YOU want it, not how OTHERS do.

☆ Practice saying 'NO'. Risk rejection.
Be clear about what you want.

☆ Examine your beliefs about what your RIGHTS, CAPABILITIES and EXPECTATIONS are.
Could they be modified?

☆ Avoid 'I AM' statements that limit you.

☆ Be your own fan club!

🦴 DEALING WITH LIFE

Life is life. It's how you SEE it that makes it DIFFICULT or EASY. Lately, you've DECIDED that it's HARD.

Happy's view:

We looked at this point in some detail in Chapter 2.

The biggest stumbling block to handling life is —

WE EXPECT THINGS TO BE PERMANENT!

It's SO OBVIOUS, but most of us still don't GET IT!

Nothing can cause greater misery than trying to fight CHANGE.

The only thing PERMANENT in life is CHANGE!

When we resist CHANGE, we expect that:

- Things should never BREAK or WEAR OUT.

- MONEY should always BE THERE.

- People's FEELINGS should never change.

- Your JOB should always be there when you WANT.

- People should never LEAVE US, GET SICK or DIE.

- We should not AGE etc.

Can you see how holding on to these expectations leads to DISAPPOINTMENT, FRUSTRATION, RESENTMENT and SADNESS if things turn out DIFFERENTLY?

Solutions:

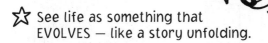

☆ See life as something that EVOLVES — like a story unfolding.

☆ Expect CHANGE and learn to roll with it.

☆ Reduce your EXPECTATIONS about how things SHOULD be.

☆ One door closes, another opens. Explore other possibilities.

PHYSICAL FACTORS

Certain PHYSICAL FACTORS can contribute to feelings of Depression, or can mimic Depression.

It is a good idea to get a PHYSICAL CHECK UP to discount any physical imbalance.

FACTORS MAY INCLUDE:

HORMONAL CHANGES

PMS, PREGNANCY and MENOPAUSE can all affect you emotionally.

DIETARY IMBALANCE

JUNK FOOD, OVEREATING, DIETING or a lack of certain NUTRIENTS can take their toll.

After all, FOOD is FUEL.

LACK OF EXERCISE

INACTIVITY can contribute greatly to a feeling of FLATNESS. Not only does your BODY run down, your MIND does too.

BURNOUT

OVERWORKING can mean little REST, POOR EATING HABITS, and a flood of STRESS CHEMICALS.

PRESCRIPTION DRUGS

ALL drugs have SIDE-EFFECTS — even over-the-counter drugs like COLD PILLS etc.

RECREATIONAL DRUGS

While drugs like ALCOHOL may give you a temporary lift, they will tend to EXAGGERATE an existing emotional state.

ILLNESS

ILLNESS, MEDICAL PROCEDURE or MEDICATION can mimic Depression.

Naturally, CHRONIC, DISABLING OR TERMINAL ILLNESS arouses deep emotions.

AGEING

Lack of general FITNESS, the chronic effects of an UNHEALTHY LIFESTYLE and the EMOTIONAL changes of AGEING can Depress you.

 WORKING SOLUTIONS

☆ PMS — Keep a chart for several months to see if there is a correlation between mood swings and menstruation, if so, PMS may be a problem.

☆ PREGNANCY — Your body goes through HUGE changes during pregnancy and childbirth. BE INFORMED, SEEK SUPPORT.

MENOPAUSE   You may need to change your
 lifestyle and diet. You may need
hormone replacement or natural
alternatives. BECOME INFORMED.

 DIET   Would you expect your car to run
efficiently on inferior or polluted
fuel? It's the same for your body.
 BALANCE your diet — less FAT, more
whole grain, vegies and fruit.

EXERCISE   Simply walking for 1/2 hr 3 times a
week not only increases your
 physical fitness, but has been
proven to lift your spirits too.

BURNOUT   Is that PROMOTION, NEW TOY,
or EXTRA MONEY more important
than your LIFE?

Have a big think about your
priorities.

 PRESCRIPTION   READ the literature. Find out what
DRUGS   you are putting in your body.

RECREATIONAL   You know the dangers.
DRUGS   Are you prepared to take the
risks? Remember — too much of
 anything still ends up being TOO
MUCH.

☆ ILLNESS

- Being AWARE of the effects of certain treatments and medications can prepare you for the symptoms.
  Try to remain DETACHED.

- Coping with disability or serious illness can be difficult. ASK for support. TALK through your feelings.

☆ AGEING

You may need to REJUVENATE your life!

- Change your hairstyle.

- Refresh your wardrobe.

- Do something you've always wanted to do.

- You may need to RETHINK your philosophy — valuing things like WISDOM, INNER BEAUTY, LOVE and FREEDOM.

9

OFF TO THE VETS

CHOOSING PROFESSIONAL HELP

Recruiting PROFESSIONAL HELP can be a valuable step in your journey out of Depression, WHETHER or NOT you are making PROGRESS yourself.

IF YOU ARE NOT MAKING HEADWAY, A GOOD THERAPIST CAN:

☆ BE A SOURCE OF EMPATHY, SUPPORT AND UNDERSTANDING.

☆ CREATE A SAFE, NON-JUDGEMENTAL ENVIRONMENT FOR YOU TO EXPRESS YOUR THOUGHTS AND FEELINGS.

☆ BE A SOURCE OF MOTIVATION AND HOPE.

☆ ASSIST YOU IN TAKING THE FIRST STEPS TO RECOVERY.

IF YOU ARE MAKING PROGRESS, A GOOD THERAPIST CAN:

☆ SUPPORT, ENCOURAGE AND STRENGTHEN YOUR PROGRESS.

☆ PROVIDE DEEPER INSIGHTS INTO PATTERNS, STICKING POINTS etc. FROM ANOTHER PERSPECTIVE.

☆ SUPPORT YOU THROUGH TIMES OF SETBACK.

☆ ASSIST YOU IN EXPLORING, UNDERSTANDING AND RELEASING THE PAST.

☆ FORTIFY YOUR SELF-ESTEEM.

☆ GUIDE YOU IN LIFE SKILLS, STRESS MANAGEMENT AND RELAXATION TECHNIQUES.

Who can help?

A trusted FRIEND, FAMILY MEMBER, SCHOOLMATE or WORK COLLEAGUE may provide the support you need, but if they can't, you may need a PROFESSIONAL. Among those who are TRAINED to assist people in crisis are:

SOCIAL WORKERS

DOCTORS

NURSES

PRIESTS OR MINISTERS OF RELIGION

CRISIS LINE COUNSELLORS

NATURAL PRACTITIONERS

ALL OF THESE PEOPLE HAVE HAD, AS PART OF THEIR TRAINING, BASIC OR ADVANCED COUNSELLING, LISTENING SKILLS AND PROBLEM-SOLVING TECHNIQUES.

For DEEPER WORK, there are:

PROFESSIONAL COUNSELLORS

They provide all of the above, only to a more advanced level.

TRAINING COURSE(S)

PSYCHOLOGISTS

They explore the mental make-up of a person and how this causes certain behaviour.

UNIVERSITY or POSTGRAD Degree or Diploma

PSYCHIATRISTS

They examine the role of the SUBCONSCIOUS in relation to behaviour.

MEDICAL DEGREE THEN SPECIALIST DEGREE IN MENTAL HEALTH

PSYCHO-THERAPISTS

They employ specialised therapies (e.g. GESTALT, NLP, BODY WORK etc.)

TRAINING IN SPECIFIC FIELD(S)

What to choose:

PSYCHIATRY tends to involve a long-term commitment with regular visits. It explores your childhood in depth.

PSYCHOLOGY can be short or long term. It will be more based in the present.

COUNSELLING involves active listening, understanding and non-intrusive guidance.

PSYCHOTHERAPY is a broad field, incorporating anything from quieter to more cathartic techniques. It can involve regular sessions or (for example) weekend intensives.

Who to choose:

The relationship between a therapist and client is a very intimate and special one.

In order to heal, you will be encouraged to express a lot of your hidden feelings, fears, hopes and dreams.

Therefore a therapist/client relationship should involve TRUST, UNDERSTANDING, HONESTY, SUPPORT, LACK OF JUDGEMENT and SAFETY.

SO, SHOP AROUND!

Not all therapists, or indeed, therapies may suit you.

You have EVERY RIGHT to ask questions and explore options to make the best choice.

MEDICATION

You can work through
Depression WITH drugs
or WITHOUT.

In fact, even if untreated, Depression will often eventually lift.

Your decision (and it is YOUR decision) to take medication if it is recommended by your GP or therapist is best made only if you are fully informed.

QUESTIONS TO ASK

⭐ WHAT WILL THE MEDICATION DO?

⭐ WHAT ARE THE SIDE EFFECTS?

⭐ HOW LONG BEFORE THE MEDICATION TAKES EFFECT?
(Some antidepressants take time to take effect.)

⭐ WHAT IS INVOLVED IN COMING OFF THE MEDICATION?

⭐ WHAT ARE THE OTHER OPTIONS?

⭐ ARE THERE ANY PRECAUTIONS? (e.g. certain foods, alcohol etc.)

IMPORTANT!

If you are taking medication, DO NOT SUDDENLY STOP! Consult your doctor or therapist before ceasing medication. You may need to be WEANED off the drug slowly.

CHOOSING THE DRUG FREE OPTION

You may wish to work through your Depression
WITHOUT medication.

If so, you will need to:

☆ IDENTIFY THE FACTORS IN YOUR LIFE THAT HAVE
CONTRIBUTED TO YOUR DEPRESSION

☆ RE-EVALUATE, CHANGE OR REMOVE AS MANY OF
THESE AS POSSIBLE

☆ BE PREPARED TO MAKE RECOVERY A PRIORITY OVER
COMFORT FOR A WHILE

☆ BE PREPARED TO RISK REJECTION, LACK OF SECURITY
etc. WHILE YOU MAKE CHANGES

☆ BECOME WELL INFORMED ABOUT DEPRESSION,
PERSONAL DEVELOPMENT etc. (THIS BOOK SHOULD
HELP!)

☆ BE VERY TRUTHFUL WITH YOURSELF AND OTHERS
ABOUT PATTERNS, ISSUES etc.

☆ BE OPEN ABOUT YOUR FEELINGS, NEEDS etc.

☆ SET GOALS FOR YOURSELF (AND REWARDS FOR
ACHIEVING THEM!).

YOU MAY NEED MEDICATION IF:

☆ YOU ARE OVERWHELMED TO THE POINT OF IMMOBILITY

☆ YOUR DEPRESSION IS CLEARLY OF A BIOLOGICAL
NATURE

☆ YOUR MOOD SWINGS ARE EXTREME

☆ YOU NEED 'TIME OUT' FROM YOUR DISTRESS IN ORDER
TO GAIN A BETTER PERSPECTIVE.

For deep or persistant Depression, MEDICATION combined with THERAPY may be the best option.

The reason for this is that while MEDICATION may provide PHYSICAL RELIEF, the PSYCHOLOGICAL or LIFESTYLE FACTORS that have contributed to your Depression will need to be addressed for there to be LONG-TERM IMPROVEMENT.

Think of it THIS WAY

Say your CAR is running low on OIL

MEDICATION may work in a similar way as covering over the WARNING LIGHT ...

...but sooner or later, you're going to need to attend to that OIL if you want your car to run well!

MEDICATION is best seen as a TEMPORARY option, to give you some SPACE and DISTANCE from the problem, so that you may view it more OBJECTIVELY and attend to what you need to.

Finally . . .

Seeking help is NOT a sign
of WEAKNESS or FAILURE!

You got into this situation because, up till now, you
did not KNOW the life skills that would prevent
this from occurring.

In fact, it is a STRONG person who
acknowledges and expresses their vulnerability
to another and a truly COURAGEOUS person who is
prepared to honestly face and CHANGE the
elements in his/her life that are not working well.

Now and then, we ALL need help.

☆ If your PIPES are leaking, you call a PLUMBER!

☆ If your WIRES are shorting, you call an ELECTRICIAN!

☆ If you can't work your COMPUTER, you'd ask
   someone who knows how, to help you!

Human beings are COMPLEX
creatures.

Sometimes we get so stuck in
ourselves we need someone else
to provide another view.

NO SHAME IN THAT!

10

THE BLACK DOG
AND THE
BLACK HOLE

WHEN THERE SEEMS NO HOPE

AND NO POINT

No book dealing with the subject of Depression can overlook the kind of despair that leads to suicidal thoughts or even suicide attempts.

This is indeed, a common aspect of Depression. You can reach a point where you feel ...

SO STUCK THAT THERE
SEEMS NO WAY OUT

THE PAIN OF DYING IS BRIEF,
THE PAIN OF LIVING GOES ON
AND ON

SO ALONE AND UNLOVED
THAT YOUR LEAVING WOULD
BE NO BIG DEAL

THAT YOU ARE JUST A
BURDEN ON OTHERS AND
THEY'D BE BETTER OFF
WITHOUT YOU

THAT THOSE WHO HURT YOU
MIGHT FINALLY UNDERSTAND
THE SUFFERING THEY CAUSED
YOU IF YOU CHECKED OUT!

While reaching such a state indicates that you are, indeed, suffering a great deal, the REALITY may not be what you think!

Let's take a look —

1. WHEN YOU HAVE A COLD, YOU SNEEZE. SNEEZING IS A SYMPTOM OF A COLD. WHEN YOU HAVE DEPRESSION, THINGS LOOK BLEAK. IT'S A SYMPTOM OF DEPRESSION. YOUR DEPRESSION IS THE REAL PROBLEM, NOT YOUR LIFE!

2. WHAT YOU'RE PERCEIVING IS NOT NECESSARILY TRUE. IT'S JUST HOW IT SEEMS BECAUSE YOU'RE DEPRESSED AT THE MOMENT.

3. THE THINGS IN YOUR LIFE ARE BEING COLOURED BY YOUR EMOTIONS. YOU'RE NOT ABLE TO SEE GOOD STUFF, BUT THAT DOESN'T MEAN IT'S NOT THERE!

4. AND EVEN IF THINGS ARE PRETTY ROTTEN, YOU'LL HAVE A BETTER CHANCE OF DEALING WITH THEM IF YOU GET YOUR DEPRESSION SORTED!

REMEMBER:

It's not a good idea to make a PERMANENT DECISION based on a TEMPORARY EMOTIONAL STATE! (even if it's dragged on for a while).

And death is VERY VERY permanent!

ASK YOURSELF —

★ Have I REALLY explored ALL of my options, sought the RIGHT HELP, WORKED on my problems?

★ What would be the REAL impact of my death on others? (Not the fantasised one.)

★ Is there REALLY no hope, or have I just lost sight of it?

★ If nobody CARES, have I given them a CHANCE to? Have I told them how I REALLY feel? Have I asked for help in a CLEAR and DIRECT way?

★ If the ones I love were SUFFERING would I want them to DIE to ease *my* burden?

If you are still considering this decision, then know that you are NOT WELL at the moment, and if you're NOT COPING you need HELP to handle this!

BOTTOM LINE —

TELL SOMEONE! ASK FOR HELP!

☆ Call TELEPHONE COUNSELLING

☆ Call a FRIEND

☆ Call a FAMILY MEMBER

☆ Call a TEACHER, MINISTER, COUNSELLOR.

Think again
Hang on

☆ You may have lost HOPE, but there's always the HOPE of finding HOPE.

☆ You don't know what's next in the script! You're just stuck in the DRAMA! Read on — the NEXT PAGES could be ...

11

NEW TRICKS

KEEPING RECOVERY
ON TRACK

There's on old saying —
'YOU CAN'T TEACH AN
OLD DOG NEW TRICKS!'
Well, since CAN'T is
one of those negative,
limiting words that
you're learning to avoid
(along with 'SHOULD' etc.)
We'll swap it for —

'YOU CAN TEACH AN OLD
DOG NEW TRICKS —
IT MIGHT JUST TAKE A
BIT LONGER!'

And, learning any
new skill involves
TIME, PATIENCE,
PERSEVERENCE and
LEARNING FROM
MISTAKES!

Changing a LIFETIME
of PATTERNS is going to
require a FOCUSED
EFFORT over a PERIOD
OF TIME.

For a while, as is true when trying anything
new, it may feel a bit uncomfortable, silly, or
unnatural, to be CHECKING IN ON YOURSELF and
CORRECTING yourself all the time.

And now and then —

YOU MIGHT FALL DOWN!

USE SETBACKS AS A TOOL

Usually, a SETBACK is going to give you a VITAL CLUE as to HOW you got stuck and HOW to PROCEED.

ASK YOURSELF:

⭐ Am I RERUNNING the past?

⭐ Am I stuck on old HURT?

⭐ Have I had enough REST?

⭐ Am I in a RUT?

⭐ What needs my ATTENTION?

⭐ What am I TELLING myself?

AND, AS THE OLD SONG GOES:

♪ PICK YOURSELF UP, ♪
DUST YOURSELF OFF,
AND *START ALL*
OVER AGAIN...

This may feel like a DRAG, but remember ...

⭐ Each small VICTORY adds up to SUCCESS

⭐ You are STRENGTHENING yourself against having to ever REPEAT this again

⭐ You are LEARNING! You are gaining WISDOM

⭐ You are creating a RESPECT for yourself that others will come to see, too.

GIVE IT TIME
GIVE IT YOUR BEST

YOU ARE RECLAIMING YOUR LIFE
And one day ...